ebony ink

written by mrc

about ebony ink

i started writing after i graduated high school in 2015. it began with journaling and documenting my emotions as i went through a post-high school transition in my life. i met the love of my life that year. as the years past, i experienced my first break up and didn't know how to cope with it. i turned to toxic friends and ignored my grief. a loved one went to heaven and i hit rock bottom. during this time, my journaling transitioned to poetry. i was too scared to get help or tell anyone. the number of emotions and pain i kept in spilled out in the language of poetry. it was the only thing that kept me going, without even understanding why i did it. one day, i decided to tell someone about my pain. from there, i said goodbye to toxic friends, healed, fell in love with my first love (again), reconnected with old friends, met new ones, learned how to love in so many different ways, grew, created, explored, changed and got engaged. to this day, i have continued to write and i will never stop. ebony ink is the 5-year journey from my lowest to my happiest. this is my way of honoring my past, a thank you to my pain, a hello to a new chapter and hug from me to you.

much love
m

table of contents

I. poems about you   1

II. heartbreak   23

III. pain   48

IV. enemies   56

V. work in progress   65

VI. beauty   77

VII. her   84

I

poems about you

i did not write it down, the day we met. i wish i did, but i'm glad i didn't. that march afternoon when the sun shined perfectly and the air was not too cool or too hot; i did not write it down. when i turned around to see a single sunflower with a piece of tissue wrapped around its stem just for me; i did not write it down. i touched its petals, smelled it's scent as it triggered an electrifying thrill throughout my spirit, i knew my life will never be the way it was. it was the birth of the most glorious and most painful adventure for my heart to take on. but, i did not write it down. feeling like ecstasy, i walked around those high school hallways like it was the streets of heaven. my feet, light as air. suddenly, everything that had meaning, didn't. everything that existed, didn't. every noise that surrounded me was put on mute and everything that had motion froze. i have not even seen your face yet, and i was already struck, melted and captivated. and yet, i did not write it down. my mind was locked down, wired, focused and desperate to know who you are. it raced and it searched for your fingerprints. and as it did, i began to imagine my life with you. what monsters will we battle and what will our victory song sound like if we win? will i be exploring the edges of the earth with you? witness dusk and dawn with you? shed blood and tears with you? what will they think now that i walk through my life while holding your hand? my brain shifted and twirled into a concoction of fear and fireworks. still, i did not write it down. i went to sleep that night knowing that you would reveal yourself to me when i wake. the moon had no control over me, for i was awake and beaming even at night. it was more than butterflies.

it was a flare of yellow sunlight filling every inch of my body. from my chest to the smile on my face, i have never felt joy like this. and still, i did not write it down. i woke the next day, without fear. there was a peace that covered me and told me that everything is happening the way it's supposed to be happening, and then i saw you. you were a stranger to my eyes, but that day, you were glowing. that smile from across the room tugged on me and i felt a sense of destiny. i tried to refuse, but the tugging turned into a clear revelation, and still, i did not write it down. i looked forward, and there you were. our eyes met and at that moment, i knew. i heard you say my name for the first time and in your tone, there was kindness and grace. you emitted a warmness that spread when we talked. we stepped back and there was a flicker of sparks. a flame lit inside me as you walked away. it was a flame of destiny and a flame of sin. i was setting myself on fire, but i believed this flame was a flame of purpose too. the voice that spoke to me, i listened. in it's whisper, i surrendered. when i swung my arms open, deep down inside me, i felt blank pages being filled with ink for the first time. it was then, i made the biggest decision of my life; to let be. i didn't write it down because it was written for us. to be written by god, the most beautiful poem? i couldn't have written it down. you were sent from heaven. i did not write it down, the day we met. i wish i did, but i'm glad i didn't.

it started with a sunflower

i can bottle up the happiness i've felt
that summer night
and it will still be sweeter
than all the wine i've tasted
in my entire lifetime

soar through
an empty highway
burst into the beaming colors
of the setting sun
into the gust of warm wind
air fills empty lungs
away we go
towards the unknown
together
we flee
dangerous and free

you're my favorite thing to write about
it's never a dull color
when you're seeping through the pages

you fill me
and mix me up inside
i rise to the rim
and overflow

you ignite fireworks
and calm storms in me

i don't mind
falling for you again
at least the view is great
on the way down

north was the city lights; sparkling and bright enough to cast a reflection on the lake below. faintly, the sounds of the freeway can be heard from a distance. the mumbles of speeding cars sounded like the turbulence of fifteen airplanes or a massive ufo racing towards us. south was complete darkness. only shadows of hills, power lines, and trees. below us was dirt. it crunched when car tires skid and as our feet danced through it. above was orion and it's million siblings on a big blanket of 11 pm blue. it was like glitter across the sky, like a glimpse of heaven. around us was complete silence. not a car horn or a whisper of a stranger was heard. only the chilling winter winds and the sound of his smooth voice. our chests against each other, getting toastier by the second. it was warm like the scent of a campfire in the summer. as he spoke, i looked to the sky and saw the beauty we're living in called life. a life of pain and of blessings. as i felt the oxygen passing through my lungs, i am reminded that i am alive, but at this moment, i am living. we were on top of the world with everything we need at our fingertips. we were spinning on saturn's rings; drowsy but awestruck. In pitch darkness, the light of the city hit my face and he saw me.

we spoke without moving our lips. he understood my words and i understood his. it was in his eyes, hidden in the darkness, i got lost in a trance and returned home at the same time. it was in his arms, i felt love: tangible. for a split second, we traveled past the atmospheres of planet earth and into the universe; where discoveries and beauties are endless. where there is stillness and sacred peace. "a little longer" he whispered. as he did, my heart asked a question and made a wish; "if perfection doesn't exist, why am i here? if only our little longer was forever. if only i can wake up next to him."

mars

the world was high speed but it slowed into a glistening spiral of silky saturated color. the stars lit up and the moon smiled. and with a touch of your hand, a fresh breeze of wind filled my lungs and danced through my hair. it was neon. it was clarity to the senses. is this what falling in love feels like? like a stream of golden light bolting through your veins? like the celestial scents of the summertime? like the peacefulness of the coast? i've landed in a world where i can swim in bliss and run in freedom, safe and sound in the honey warmth of your arms. persistence like the strongest stone. joy like the rising of the sun. you're a rush of rainbow and a million other colors unknown to man, and still, no poem can paint the love you've lavished upon me. it's you, isn't it? it's almost as if we're forever.

love

in a world of such despair
even if we did part
we discovered the light in it
and we found it together

how foolish is it
to fall into love with another castaway?
to walk blindly with the blind?
call it twisted
but i'd say it's loneliest of voids
to be without a friend
than to be alone

lost together

214 is tattooed to my brain
it hurts so much
but i'm in love with this pain
i'm in love with your t-shirt scent
it's summer
but i'm drowning in february rain

i wish the seconds felt like hours
peppermint and steam were filling the showers
but i didn't mind
it felt like home
like it was ours

still have the wine stain spills
and advil pills
i keep things that remind me of you
because it contains the thrill
i never want to forget
so i bury you in my head like a drill

i remember when you called me your wife
and it stung like a knife
when i saw my own life without you in it
i guess you're my drug
you make it hard to quit it

i miss you most when the moon's out
do you feel me
trembling through your skin?
i know you dream of me too

you're spiraling under a spell
collapsing in the weak of your bones
like zero gravity on earth
i'll fly you to the stars
with your feet to the ground

please look into my eyes
and make love to me
like we're waltzing on the stars
rock me till i off the edge of no control
you're a mix of sensuality and magic
fill me up
till i burst
all i want is you

you asked me to be your wife
and my heart sunk to the floor
as i see the hell we came out of
the paradise we're in
and the heaven we'll make

these scars we share
this kiss will stain

august 1

II

heartbreak

i am not going to tell you
that your hands have been
choking the life out of me
leave me bleed
i just want to see you smile
even if it sacrifices
my own

your love is
venomous
disguised as an
antidote

i mishear warning sirens for fairytale chimes

you
both
the storm
and the shelter
the murder house
and the hospital

i need to spill my truth
before i drown in it
before i bring you down with it

if you have the power
to pull me out of hell
you can pull yourself out too

promise me
even in your changing seasons
will you still look at me
and see summer?

remember the fear of breaking apart
and the piercing truth
of it being the only option?
the mess that we made
was the mess that we were

you loved me enough
to leave yourself drowning
so that i can reach the surface

i wish we lived in a world
where i can love you
and it will be okay

you're fading
you're dimming from my sight
i want to be lavished in color
but all you give me is transparency

i used to call you home
but the truth is
i feel homesick when i am with you
i am stranger walking into cold, unfamiliar arms

i don't know
how many words i'll have to write
to forget one
your name

now as the sun sets
you aren't on my mind
the night once sparked
the desire of your presence
your silky touch of hand
and the honey warmth of your skin
only you
i wanted
now my mind replaces you
with an image i created
he's what you aren't
he did what you didn't
i love him
as much as i wish you would

covet

it's hard to have faith
when you lied to me
numb yourself up
then hide from me

wounds

i'm sinking in love for you
please believe me when i say
i care about you

i don't want your hands on mine
my head tilts right while you drive
LA's nice
but the music's loud
i miss the shores to the clouds
busy buzzing from my phone
where are you?
when are you coming home?
i don't know anymore
you're too much to ignore
i'm too busy stretching myself out
so you won't feel so sore
in your arms, i felt so safe
at least not anymore
how many shots for me to take
till i leave right your through doors?

will i ever feel again?
will the july sunshine ever feel the same on my skin?
wish i'd corkscrewed it
before it went old
feel me now
i'm december cold
stuck in red roses
gripped to summer gold

i don't speak of my doubts because if i do they'll be true
am i afraid of the truth
or the fear of losing you?
am i afraid of unhappiness
or someone else loving you?

can't you try?
i've been dragging chains so you'll get by
bleed for you then watch you cry
if i were you
you'd try a million times
now you're drowning
and i'm running dry
can't you try?

they never believe me when i say
you're just as perfect as you are
it's all tricks and games they'll say
but can they fathom
the wonder of
discovering a gem
in a vast, hopeless desert
gems aren't extinct
they're just in few
but i was lucky enough to find you
and you were
brave enough
to come out from hiding
there is a strength
i see in you
that binds wounds together
a fluorescence
that magnetizes and leads

a tenderness
that loves and gives unceasingly
a curiosity
that contemplates then creates
but somehow
it is not enough for you
when i watch you grow
there is a doubt that boils inside
that i might wake up one day
and see a stranger laying next to me
my faith shakes at your lips
my hope dissolves
as you speak your truth
i fell into love with you
only for you become someone else
why must you change

please, don't change

sometimes
love is so relentless
it floods not just one
but all

is it true that i need you?
if i go will chase me?
am i worth more than pennies and diamonds
and every mile that stretches the sea?

III

pain

i fell asleep
but woke up
in an aftermath
if i was sleeping through the storm
tell me why
everything is covered
in my fingerprints

you think i am free
because freedom to you sparkles like gold
not only the jewels upon my neck
sparkle and shine
but so does the bars of my prison cell

shall i follow your voice
or the hope of your response?
the silent sounds of you
are loud enough for me
where have you been?
where do i go?
what do i do?
i can't go much further
if the silent sounds from you
just a whisper
just one hum
just sing me
one of your songs
just let me know
if you are still there
before i go
before i give you up

the silent sounds of you

to be full and empty
lost and found
at the same time
to come to the highest
but to drop back down
should i keep going
if my happiness might not meet me there?

i was there
plunged at the bottom of the sea
walking in circles
with stones to my ankles
raw desperateness
i let out at cry for help
to the sky
in pitch silence
i opened my mouth and began to sing
the last few drops of oxygen left in my lungs
was used as a surrender
but i would be lying
if i said i was singing to myself
i would be on my deathbed
if was alone that night
but i wasn't
i was not alone

Rock bottom

if
there's
no
pain
in
heaven
why
won't
you
take
me
there

i'm a solo runner
being chased
i can't turn my head to check
who is behind me
i can't squint my eyes
far enough
to see the finish line
cheerleaders on the sidelines
they tell me i'll be okay
their smiles
mock me
and make me sick to my stomach
do they know how i feel?
do they know what it's like
to chase
and to be chased?

anxiety

IV

enemies

you put my name
on your emotions
because you're afraid
of your own

i can't be your mirror
just because yours is shattered

insecure

she was lonely enough
to lie in my ears
jealous enough
to celebrate my tears
people like them
never apologize
for misery loves company
just as
jealousy loves revenge

slither

your sins and deceptions
found its way inside me
and the toxicity of your words
taught me how to hate just like you
why drag me
into your pit of heartlessness
and make pretend
its a paradise?

you hurt me the most
but i still want you alive
i only wish death
to your demons inside

is this what empathy feels like?

years from now
when you tell the world what i've done
it's up to them to choose
because only bitter hearts
act on revenge
only the fearful
dig in the past
like picking dirt from the ground
i know the truth
and it's enough to keep my mouth
shut

there's people that hurt
but then there's evil
my father always said,
"there's a specially reserved place in hell for those people"

i'm not afraid to say
this is the happiest i've ever been
so please let me celebrate
you don't need to join in

V

work in progress

one day
you will find your true reflection
one day
you will finally look in the mirror
and see your true, divine beauty
not by the curves of your waist
or of the clothes on your body
but the light in your heart
and the detailed importance of your existence

reflection

freedom
came from someone
who decided to pick a fight
with fear
when everybody else
dared to look in its face

the only thing that grew
is the fear that you chose to water
it is no longer a seed
it has grown into a tree
for you to take refuge
in the shadows of its arms
pulling you away from the truth that is the light
and making you comfortable enough to dwell in the dark

i'm in chains
but i'm no slave
to the weight of your waves

take this pain
as rich soil
to root yourself deeper
to make your trunk stronger
and to make your fruit sweeter

it's useless
if your words
are breathing life
and your actions
are resting in peace

the rain
it's coming
it's not hope
if you don't believe
what you're becoming

i'm a spark
i'm a flame
a living testimony
death to shame
death to fear
death to pain
death to hoping for the rain
listen up
hear my chains
hit the ground
ultrasound

the birth of a new age

i'm stepping in
i'm jumping free
no hesitation
no ground below me

i will swim through the cracks you have created in my heart
i will let you play in these sacred places in my mind
i will look you in your eyes
and watch the destruction of your hands
because i let you in through my doors
but once you've had your time here
i hope you enjoyed your stay
because you will never set foot again
these gates will be locked
and these streets will be paved in solid concrete
of love and of gratitude
and by that time
i will be the queen of this land
and i will be able to love again

let your grief come and go

i'll fix my faith and see the unseen
i will keep my flame bright
not to burn others
but to live furiously free

VI

beauty

we are stars
scattered among a blank canvas called the sky
the night is alive
and never dead
because of us
solitaries
simultaneously
extraordinaries
faintly glowing in isolation
but constructing magnificence in unification
we are stars

when daughters and sons
decide to build a symphony
instead of a chaotic cacophony
destruction
becomes
resurrection

isn't it beautiful
to know that each and every person your lay eyes on
is pioneering through an adventure
just as vast
as your own?

the past is unchangeable, the future is unable to be seen. but the present is powerfully delicate. it is to be witnessed by the eyes only once, as a film without a replay button. harmoniously, like a grand commencement and a blank page, ready to be stained by permanent ink.

you're addicted to the noise
but we're in love
with the silenced peace
of our own souls

all though
the sun sets
it has never refused
to rise

VII

her

go ahead
wreck her
and make her bleed
watch her as she screams
but do you really think
it will stop her?
she will only
take her pain
and use it
to rebuild her castle
stronger than before
and after she's done
she'll use the extra pieces
to grow a garden

her touch will electrify you
and send a shock wave through your spirit
it will create
fear and bravery
confusion and clarity
all at once

i look at her
and pity me
for how selfish i am
to know that
this life i am living
is one that she has to
bleed and battle through
just to get a glimpse of

privilege

do not hesitate to give her away
what other chance will you have
to possess the rarest of diamonds
like her
ever again?

tell your daughters
they are loved
before another man
does it for you

melanin straight from the honeycombs
silky skin of gold
gracious but bold
one of the many marigolds

she will hide under mountains of mascara and lipstick
throw shade and click click
on her phone as she
post pics
here is a girl who is trapped
here is a victim
hurt by the hands of
photoshopped portraits and
misleading ads
they say
make her believe her fat is bad
she should be ashamed instead of glad
she breaks mirrors
because beauty is pain
she lowers herself because she's
not the same as the girl in reign
she doesn't have her hair, her private jet plane
so she sheds her skin to become another
fix up her features given by her mother

girls

i told myself
abandon her
to be her is to be owned by shame
that was then
in the backyard of fifteen
and in the 5 am sunrise
you loved, so you believed
your body, sanctified
but your spirit, trapped
you gave it away and left yourself dry
your tears
flowing softly
shimmering in blue
smooth like silk, pierced like knives
it was the sharp pain of
gripping onto dear life
and letting go at the same time
you injured with your words
fell short, went numb and went blind

chopped off your hair and let it consume you
erased her to be of the blueprint
you erased her so much
till you wanted to erase you
a sinister place and a curse of
unforgiveness
i am not afraid of you
i told myself
abandoning her is abandoning me
i will run beside her
and never away from her
i told myself
to be her
is an empty price tag
she is freedom beyond possession
i see you now, and it is clear
all you wanted was to
love them
but all you needed was to
love you
i watch you
shed colorful tears
blue, yellow, grey, red
crack a smile and a laugh
share hugs and throw punches
light fires and put them out
touch the sun and the ocean floor

wander vast lands
sing a thousand melodies
bond without barrier
live with gratitude
love in unity
your life is beautiful
i am not apart from you
i am you, and you are
forgiven
these silky tears
are growing a harvest of bravery
and painting a masterpiece
beyond the blueprint

thank you

thank you to my wonderful friends and the memories we share. you have become the sisters i never had. thank you to my best friend and the love of my life for relentlessly loving every inch of me. you have shown me what love is. thank you to those who aren't in my life anymore. i hope you are taking care of yourself. i hope you are happy. there is not one speck of hate in my heart for you. thank you to my mom and dad. we are not a perfect family, but without your sacrifice and your patience, i wouldn't be alive.

Lightning Source UK Ltd.
Milton Keynes UK
UKHW020957250320
360834UK00003B/160